Whisper WARRIOR

An inspirational book for girls

By: Misty Gee

Copyright © 2021 Misty Gee

Published in Montgomery, Texas

All rights reserved. No part of this publication may be reproduced, distributed, or transmitted in any form or by any means, including photocopying, recording, or other electronic or mechanical methods, without the prior written permission of the author, except in the case of brief quotations embodied in critical reviews and certain other noncommercial uses permitted by copyright law.

eBook ISBN: 978-1-7378696-0-3

Paperback ISBN: 978-1-7378696-1-0

Hardcover ISBN: 978-1-7378696-2-7

LCCN 2021919243

To my beautiful warriors,

Jasmine and Violet

Psst! Wake Up! Knock, knock!
The time has come, let's go.
Step out into the light,
and let your talents show.

You are a strong, courageous warrior,
you won't be stopped, no way.
No hiding, no worries, no fear.
Today's your special day.

Believe!

The path is all laid out.

Follow the light and use your brain.

And remember not to doubt.

Whether you turn to the left or to the right, you will surely hear a voice. "This is the way, walk in it!"
The world waits to rejoice.

Be Still!

It's time to focus on the prize.

Look inside and deep within.

That's where the magic hides.

It all works out, you'll see.
You were created for a purpose,
and will find out who you're
meant to be.

Give!

Please don't forget your heart.

You should take care of others.

Make sure to do your part.

For when you give you receive,
great things come to those who love.
Love's patient, kind, and limitless
as the skies above.

Trust!

The storms will come and go.

Stand firm, be honest, be true.

You are here for a reason.

There's nobody like you.

You are beautifully created,
from your head to your toes.
Have faith in yourself.
Remember to keep your peace,
wherever life goes.

And now, it is your turn.
This is the nudge you need.
Faint whisper to a warrior,
it's time you took the lead!

The End

www.ingramcontent.com/pod-product-compliance
Lightning Source LLC
Chambersburg PA
CBHW041109210426

43209CB00063BA/1861